★★★ AMERICAN ACHIEVEMENTS ★★★

ONE GIANT LEAP

AMERICA'S MISSION TO THE MOON

LISA IDZIKOWSKI

Lerner Publications ◆ Minneapolis

For my family

Lerner Publications Company
An imprint of Lerner Publishing Group, Inc.
241 First Avenue North
Minneapolis, MN 55401 USA

For reading levels and more information, look up this title at www.lernerbooks.com.

Main body text set in Aptifer Slab LT Pro.
Typeface provided by Linotype AG.

Editor: Brianna Kaiser **Designer:** Kimberly Morales **Photo Editor:** Lucien Brinkley
Lerner team: Sue Marquis

Library of Congress Cataloging-in-Publication Data

Names: Idzikowski, Lisa author
Title: One giant leap : America's mission to the moon / Lisa Idzikowski.
Description: Minneapolis : Lerner Publications, [2026] | Series: American achievements | Includes bibliographical references and index. | Audience: Ages 8–12 | Audience: Grades 4–6 | Summary: "When astronauts first landed and walked on the moon, it changed history. Readers will learn about the Apollo program, the people who made the first moon landing possible, and the program's lasting legacy"— Provided by publisher.
Identifiers: LCCN 2025011164 (print) | LCCN 2025011165 (ebook) | ISBN 9798765688823 library binding | ISBN 9798348028671 paperback | ISBN 9798765695463 epub
Subjects: LCSH: Project Apollo (U.S.)—Juvenile literature | Space vehicles—Landing—Moon—Juvenile literature | Moon—Exploration—Juvenile literature
Classification: LCC TL793 .I34 2025 (print) | LCC TL793 (ebook) | DDC 629.45/4—dc23/eng/20250805

LC record available at https://lccn.loc.gov/2025011164
LC ebook record available at https://lccn.loc.gov/2025011165

Manufactured in the United States of America
1-1012619-54712-4/30/2025

TABLE OF CONTENTS

CHAPTER 1

THE RACE TO FAR AWAY!

Apollo 11 launches on the morning of July 16, 1969.

Three, two, one, zero . . . all engines running. Liftoff! Millions of people watched a giant rocket blast off from the National Aeronautics and Space Administration (NASA) Kennedy Space Center in Florida. Three astronauts inside Apollo 11 sat strapped in their seats. The craft shook and rattled. Loud noise surrounded the eager space travelers.

It was July 16, 1969. People in the Launch Control Center, Mission Control Center, and around the world hoped for success. If all went well, the astronauts would land on the moon in a few days.

People in the Launch Control Center watch the Apollo 11 liftoff.

On July 20, 1969, people in astronaut Neil Armstrong's hometown of Wapakoneta, Ohio, watch Armstrong walk on the moon on a TV broadcast.

The idea of a moon mission had begun years before. It started after World War II (1939–1945). During this war, the United States and the Soviet Union—a country that broke up into fifteen countries, including Russia, in 1991—were allies. Soon after, the two countries stood on opposite sides. The United States was a democracy and wanted to protect democratic freedom around the world. The Soviet Union was Communist and wanted to spread this type of government to other countries.

Americans and Soviets competed to become the world's superpower. They spied, built up large supplies of weapons, and constructed rockets and missiles. This fierce competition became known as the Cold War (1947–1991).

A Soviet Union poster promoting the space race during the Cold War

SMALL SATELLITE, BIG SURPRISE

American scientists and engineers had already invented light bulbs, airplanes, televisions, and the atomic bomb. Many Americans believed they were the world's best in science and technology. On the evening of October 4, 1957, a major surprise shattered this belief. The Soviets had launched the first human-made satellite, the beach ball–sized Sputnik. Its small radio beeped as it orbited Earth every ninety-eight minutes.

Sputnik shocked Americans. Now they were in a space race with the Soviet Union.

A LOVE FOR SPACE

Franklin R. Chang-Díaz developed a love for space at a young age and was inspired by Sputnik. When he was eighteen, he left his home in Costa Rica and moved to the United States to study engineering and physics. He became a NASA astronaut in 1980. Chang-Díaz flew seven space shuttle missions.

Astronaut Franklin R. Chang-Díaz on a space shuttle mission in 1996

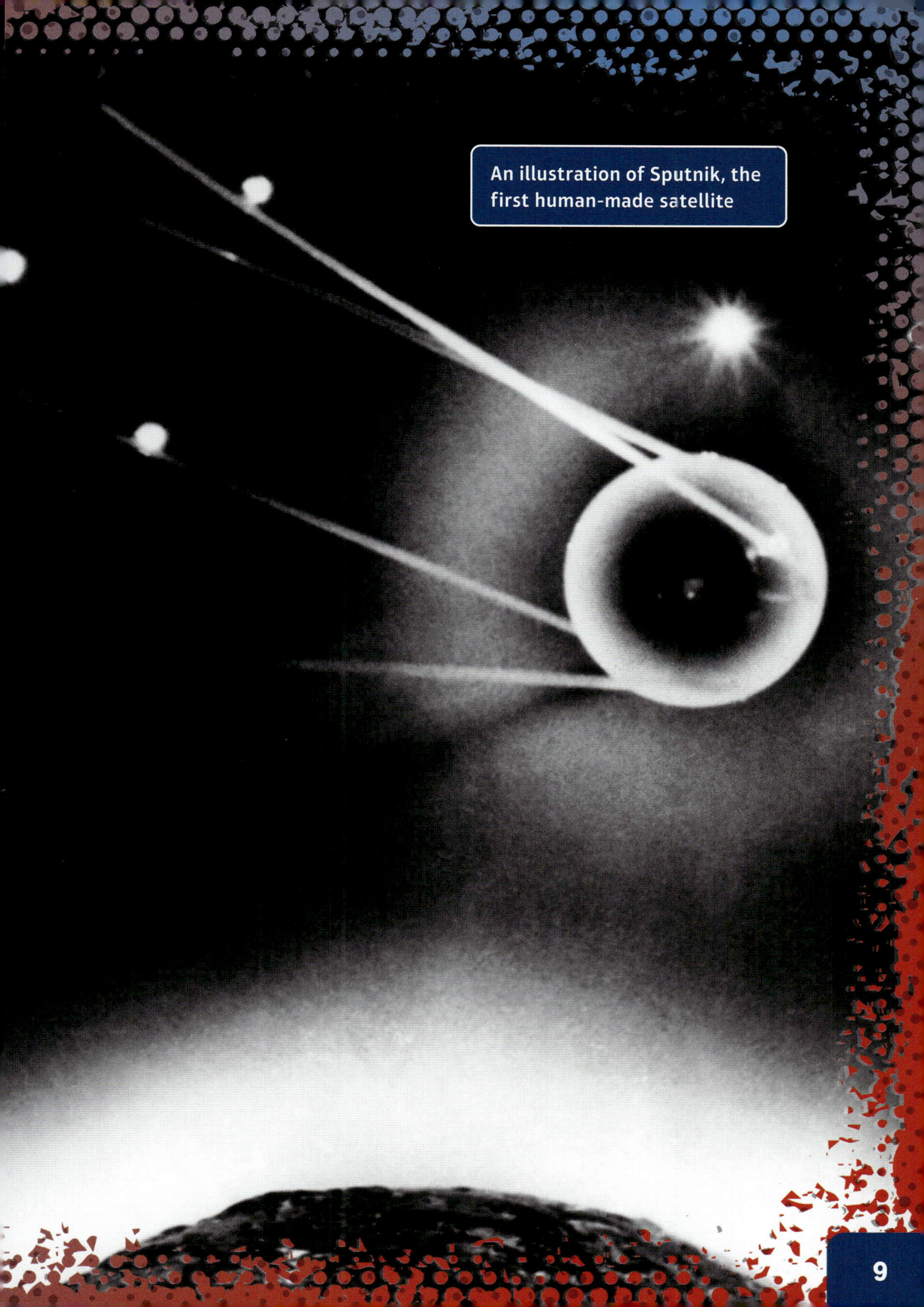

An illustration of Sputnik, the first human-made satellite

CHAPTER 2

MOON, HERE WE COME

President John F. Kennedy speaks to Congress about landing a person on the moon.

In 1961 John F. Kennedy became the president of the United States. He wanted the United States to be the first country to land a person on the moon. On May 25, 1961, Kennedy told Congress his goal of landing on the moon by the end of the decade.

Congress loved the idea. They gave Kennedy the money for his mission, known as the Moonshot. NASA began searching for the best and brightest engineers, scientists, and mathematicians to work on the Apollo program. People came from universities and businesses around the United States. More than four hundred thousand Americans worked on the Apollo program.

NASA and the world suffered hard times during the Apollo program. On November 22, 1963, Kennedy was assassinated. Four years later, the crew of Apollo 1 died during a launchpad test. America mourned, but Apollo moved ahead.

Apollo 11 commander Neil Armstrong reviewing flight plans

APOLLO CARRIES ON

On January 9, 1969, NASA announced the Apollo 11 crew. The team was made up of three experienced astronauts: commander Neil Armstrong, command module pilot Michael Collins, and lunar module pilot Edwin "Buzz" Aldrin. The astronauts trained hard for their mission. But without other hardworking people at NASA, the mission would not succeed.

The Apollo 11 crew, *left to right*: Neil Armstrong, Michael Collins, and Edwin "Buzz" Aldrin

Mathematician Katherine Johnson working at NASA in 1966

Space travel relies on engineering and math. At the time of the Apollo program, NASA had a team of mathematicians, most of them women, who were known as human computers. Katherine Johnson was one of them. She calculated flight plans for many missions, all by hand. Her calculations helped lead Apollo 11 to the moon.

PROJECT MERCURY

Project Mercury was the first human spaceflight program. In 1959 NASA chose seven astronauts to go to space. The men were military pilots. They had to meet many requirements and pass medical exams. The medical director wondered if women pilots could pass the same tests. Thirteen women, known as the Mercury 13, passed. But they never became astronauts. NASA didn't accept women as astronauts into their program until 1978.

Computers use software to function. These coded instructions keep the machines running. Computer scientist Margaret Hamilton led NASA's software team. They developed the software for Apollo's onboard flight computers.

Before they could fly a mission, the crew of astronauts had to be healthy. NASA had experts to help. Nurse Dee O'Hara helped found NASA's Flight Medicine Clinic and looked after the health of the astronauts. She gave crews their preflight and postflight physicals. She also gave checkups to the astronauts' families.

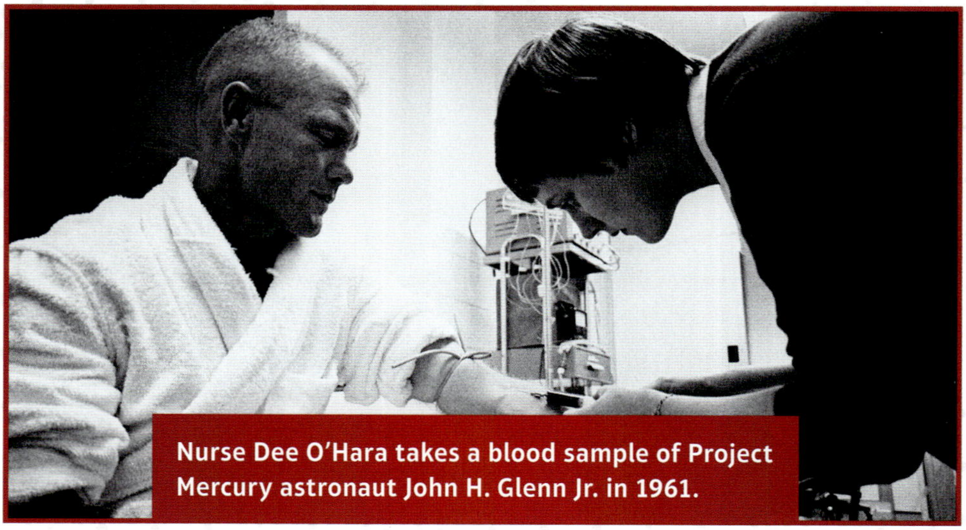

Nurse Dee O'Hara takes a blood sample of Project Mercury astronaut John H. Glenn Jr. in 1961.

Hazel Fellows sews an Apollo space suit at the International Latex Corporation in 1968.

Astronauts needed space suits to survive in space. Engineers worked with the International Latex Corporation to make the suits. Hazel Fellows, Iona Allen, and other women worked at the latex company. Fellows sewed space suits for the Apollo program from 1962 to 1974. Allen had a talent for sewing the most difficult items, and she constructed Armstrong's lunar boots.

Everyone at NASA was busy. With only months to launch Apollo 11, everyone continued to practice, plan, and prepare.

CHAPTER 3

LAUNCH TO LANDING

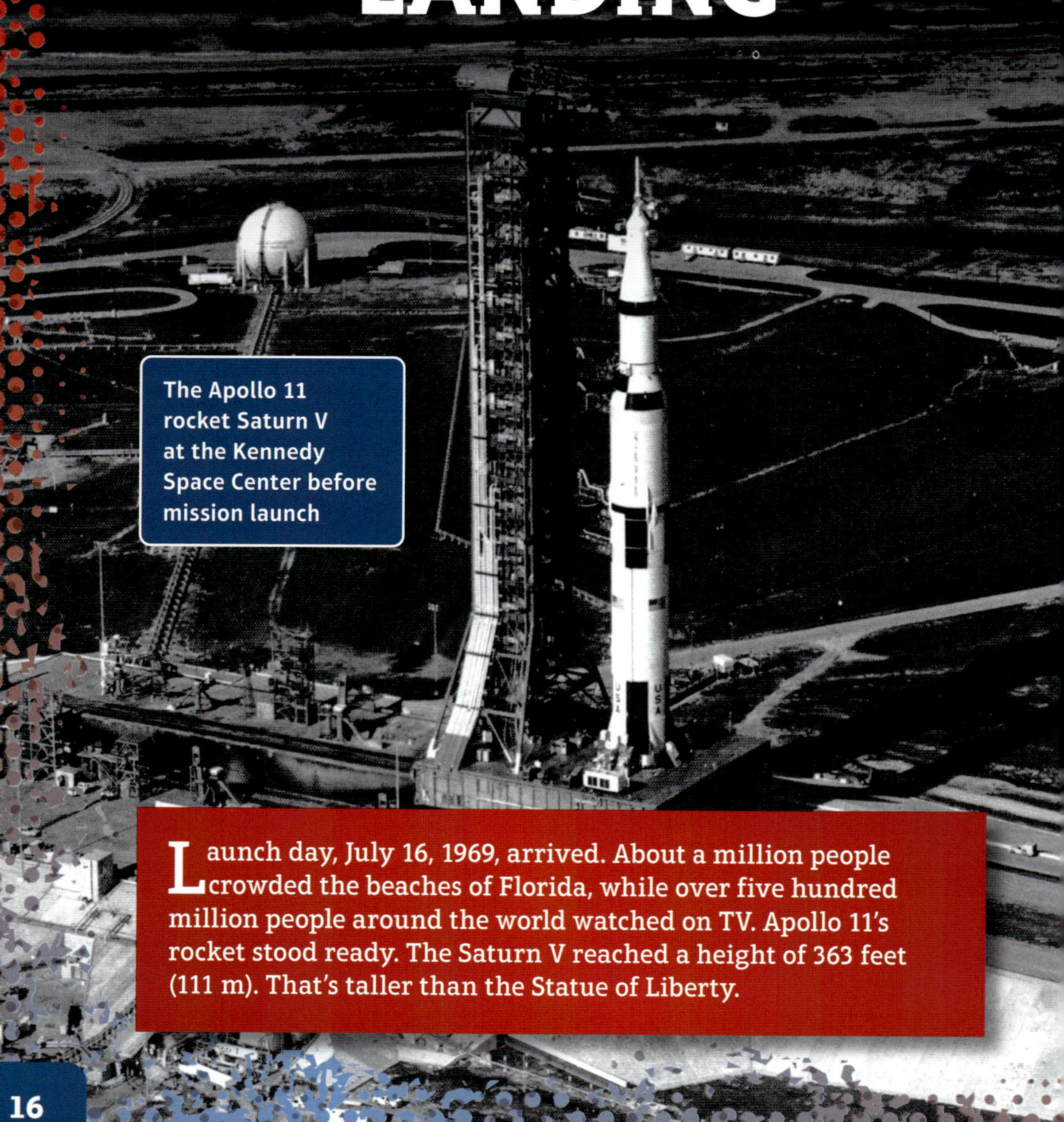

The Apollo 11 rocket Saturn V at the Kennedy Space Center before mission launch

Launch day, July 16, 1969, arrived. About a million people crowded the beaches of Florida, while over five hundred million people around the world watched on TV. Apollo 11's rocket stood ready. The Saturn V reached a height of 363 feet (111 m). That's taller than the Statue of Liberty.

Perched atop Saturn V, Apollo 11 had three parts. Armstrong, Collins, and Aldrin would live in Columbia, the command module. Inside, it was about the size of a large car. The service module provided power and stored things the astronauts would need such as oxygen. Both modules would stay connected for most of the trip. The lunar module Eagle was bug-shaped and would take the astronauts down to the moon.

A crowd in New York City's Central Park watches Armstrong become the first person to walk on the moon in 1969.

Instrumentation controller JoAnn Morgan and others in the launch firing room watch the Apollo 11 liftoff.

TIME TO GO

The astronauts rose at about 4:00 a.m. After breakfast, they dressed in their 200-pound (91-kg) space suits. Judy Sullivan, the lead biomedical engineer of the mission, helped Armstrong into his suit. A few hours later, Jack King began the countdown at the Kennedy Space Center. Instrumentation controller JoAnn Morgan was the only woman in the launch firing room.

Apollo 11 lifted off at 9:32 a.m. toward the moon. As soon as the rocket cleared the launch tower, Mission Control Center in Houston, Texas, took over.

APOLLO PROTESTS

Minister and civil rights activist Ralph Abernathy saw the billions of dollars spent on the Apollo program as a waste of money. The day before launch, he and a group of Black families protested at Kennedy Space Center. The protesters said the money should be used for feeding people on Earth and helping those in poverty instead.

Ralph Abernathy holds up a sign protesting the Apollo 11 launch.

THE FIRST MOON LANDING

On July 20, about one hundred hours since takeoff, Armstrong and Aldrin readied Eagle for landing. While Collins remained on Columbia in lunar orbit, Eagle began descending to its landing site, the Sea of Tranquility. Eagle needed a smooth place to land safely, but Armstrong saw a field of boulders instead. The commander grabbed the controls and piloted the craft. With only seconds left, he found a smooth landing spot. The Eagle touched down.

A photo taken by Armstrong showing Aldrin on the moon during the Apollo 11 mission

About four hours later, Armstrong climbed outside Eagle. He stepped down the ladder and became the first human to step onto the moon. Aldrin soon joined him.

Both astronauts had much to do. They set up an American flag and conducted experiments. One experiment measured quakes on the moon. They collected 47 pounds (21 kg) of moon rocks and snapped 166 pictures. After finishing their work, they climbed aboard Eagle, ate, and rested.

The next morning, Armstrong and Aldrin lifted off the moon. Eagle docked with Columbia. Armstrong, Aldrin, and Collins headed home. On July 24, they splashed down in the Pacific Ocean. Apollo 11 was back on Earth.

THE END OF APOLLO

After Apollo 11, five other missions landed on the moon. Apollo 17 was the last, landing on December 11, 1972. Twelve astronauts in all walked on the moon. Apollo 13 never made it to the moon. The crew survived an onboard explosion before making it safely back to Earth.

The Apollo 11 crew gets picked up after splashing down in the Pacific Ocean on July 24, 1969.

CHAPTER 4

WHAT'S UP NEXT?

The Space Launch System rocket launches with the Orion spacecraft in 2022 for the Artemis 1 mission.

NASA is planning more crewed missions to the moon with its Artemis program. These missions will develop and test new technology. Astronauts will explore more of the moon's surface. The missions will also prepare humans to live and work on the moon and prepare humans to one day travel to Mars.

The first Artemis mission was completed in 2022. This uncrewed trip tested a new rocket and spaceship. The second Artemis mission will have four crew members. They will be the first crew to orbit the moon since Apollo 17 in 1972.

The next moon landing is planned for Artemis III. Four astronauts will crew its ship. Two of them will land on the moon's south polar region.

Christina Koch (*left*), Victor Glover (*top*), Reid Wiseman (*bottom*), and Jeremy Hansen make up the Artemis II crew.

GATEWAY TO MARS

NASA is preparing for deep space investigation with Gateway. This new space station will orbit the moon. Artemis astronauts will stay there and conduct experiments. They will also use it as a launchpad to the moon's surface. Experience with these new space adventures will help NASA someday launch crewed missions to Mars.

The Orion spacecraft docks to the Gateway space station.

APOLLO'S LEGACY

The Apollo program produced many benefits for society. The technologies invented for Apollo help in everyday life. Computer systems used to fly Apollo spacecraft are like those flying today's airplanes. They also power cruise control in cars.

Apollo's guidance computer was about the size of a small suitcase and had very little memory. The newest iPhones have over a million times more memory. Space suits protected the astronauts from extreme heat. The suits were made from fireproof material. The type of insulation in space suits is now found in firefighting and camping gear.

Aldrin in front of Apollo's guidance computer

Many scientists and engineers were children when Armstrong stepped onto the moon. As a six-year-old, Mae Jemison told her kindergarten teacher that she would become a scientist. In 1992 Jemison became the first Black woman in space.

As the Artemis missions take off, more children can be inspired by astronauts walking on the moon and the people who helped them get there.

Children can be inspired by future moon missions.

Astronaut Mae Jemison working in space in 1992

MOON LANDING TIMELINE

★ **1957** The Soviets launch Sputnik, the first human-made satellite, on October 4.

★ **1959** NASA chooses seven astronauts to go to space as part of Project Mercury.

★ **1961** President John F. Kennedy tells Congress that the United States will land a man on the moon before the end of the decade.

★ **1969** Apollo 11 launches on its way to the moon on July 16.

Neil Armstrong and Buzz Aldrin walk on the moon on July 21.

Apollo 11 returns to Earth on July 24.

★ **1972** Apollo 17 becomes the last Apollo mission to land on the moon.

★ **1992** Mae Jemison becomes the first Black woman to go to space.

★ **2022** Artemis I launches, orbits the moon, and returns to Earth.

★ **2023** NASA announces the crew of Artemis II on April 3.

Astronauts attend NASA's announcement of the Artemis II crew in 2023.

GLOSSARY

activist: a person who fights for a cause

allies: to be on the same side of an argument or war; joined in an alliance

astronaut: a person who travels to outer space

cold war: a struggle between two nations with political differences

commander: a person in control or in charge

Communist: a government structure where one authoritarian party controls the state-owned means of production

democracy: a government where people have power through representation and the right to vote

mission control: people on the ground who direct the flight of a spacecraft

poverty: a low amount or lack of money

satellite: an object that orbits some other object in space

software: coded instructions that tell computers how to function

LEARN MORE

Britannica Kids: Sputnik
https://kids.britannica.com/students/article/Sputnik/585303

Mooney, Carla. *Christina Hammock Koch: Artemis Astronaut*. Lerner Publications, 2026.

NASA: Gateway Learning Resources
https://www.nasa.gov/gateway-learning-resources/

NASA: What Was the Saturn V?
https://www.nasa.gov/learning-resources/for-kids-and-students/what-was-the-saturn-v-grades-k-4/

National Geographic Kids: Katherine Johnson
https://kids.nationalgeographic.com/history/article/katherine-johnson

Pierce, Simon. *The Artemis Program*. PowerKids, 2025.

Rains, Dalton. *Apollo 11*. Apex, 2025.

Rhatigan, Joe, and Beth Adelman. *Artemis Mission: Return to the Moon*. Lerner Publications, 2024.

INDEX

PHOTO ACKNOWLEDGMENTS

Image credits: NASA/Project Apollo Archive, pp. 4, 20, 25; NASA/KSC, p. 5; AP Photo/Bill Sauro, p. 6; Photo 12/Alamy, p. 7; NASA, pp. 8, 11, 12, 14, 16, 18, 21; ullstein bild via Getty Images, p. 9; Arnie Sachs/CNP/Getty Images, p. 10; NASA/Bob Nye, p. 13; NASA/Smithsonian National Air and Space Museum, p. 15; AP Photo, p. 17; Bettmann/Getty Images, p. 19; NASA/Keegan Barber, p. 22; NASA/Josh Valcarcel, p. 23; NASA/Alberto Bertolin/Bradley Reynolds, p. 24; Dana Neibert/Getty Images, p. 26; NASA/MSFC, p. 27; MARK FELIX/AFP via Getty Images, p. 29. Design elements: Sanches11/Shutterstock; Mooam/Shutterstock; brwen/Shutterstock.
Cover: NASA/Project Apollo Archive.

Greatest of All Time College Sports

G.O.A.T. College Football Players

Beth Adelman

Lerner Publications ◆ Minneapolis

Stats in this book are accurate through the 2024 college football season.

Lerner Publications Company
An imprint of Lerner Publishing Group, Inc.
241 First Avenue North
Minneapolis, MN 55401 USA

For reading levels and more information, look up this title at www.lernerbooks.com.

Main body text set in Aptifer Sans LT Pro.
Typeface provided by Linotype.

Library of Congress Cataloging-in-Publication Data

Names: Adelman, Beth, author.
Title: G.O.A.T. college football players / Beth Adelman.
Other titles: Greatest-of-all-time college football players
Description: Minneapolis : Lerner Publications , 2026. | Series: Lerner sports. Greatest of all time college sports | Includes bibliographical references and index. | Audience: Ages 7–11 | Audience: Grades 2–3 | Summary: “College football is incredibly popular in the US, and fans love to follow its biggest superstars. Meet the ten best college football players of all time, then rank them yourself!”—Provided by publisher.
Identifiers: LCCN 2024044922 (print) | LCCN 2024044923 (ebook) | ISBN 9798765668559 (library binding) | ISBN 9798765684177 (paperback) | ISBN 9798765677735 (epub)
Subjects: LCSH: Football players—United States—Biography—Juvenile literature. | Football players—Rating of—United States—Juvenile literature. | College sports—United States—Juvenile literature.
Classification: LCC GV939.A1 A345 2026 (print) | LCC GV939.A1 (ebook) | DDC 796.33092/2 [B]—dc23/eng/20250122

LC record available at https://lccn.loc.gov/2024044922
LC ebook record available at https://lccn.loc.gov/2024044923

Manufactured in the United States of America
1-1011443-53823-4/23/2025

TABLE OF CONTENTS

Alabama freshman Tua Tagovailoa (right) throws a pass in the 2018 national title game against the Georgia Bulldogs.

Victory!

The University of Alabama was down 13–0 in the 2018 National Collegiate Athletic Association (NCAA) football title game. Their desperate coach sent in the backup quarterback—freshman Tua Tagovailoa. In overtime, the University of Georgia scored a field goal. Alabama needed a touchdown to win. Tagovailoa got sacked for a loss of yards. But on the next play, he threw the football 41 yards down the field. DeVonta Smith caught it and scored for Alabama. Victory!

Almost 150 years before, in 1869, Rutgers and Princeton Universities played the first college football game. Rutgers won 6–4. Back then, a touchdown was two points, and a field goal was five points. The field was 20 yards longer and 46.6 yards wider than it is today.

This statue at Rutgers University honors the first college football game.

The first footballs were made from pigs' bladders. The balls were round and heavy. Players mostly kicked them. In 1874, a lighter ball was introduced, making passing easier. But forward passes were not allowed. They could only throw the ball behind the line of scrimmage. Players mostly ran with the ball.

US president Theodore Roosevelt was a big football fan. But the game was so rough that many players were hurt. A few even died. Roosevelt insisted football be made safer.

FACTS AT A GLANCE

- Only one player has won the Heisman Trophy twice. Archie Griffin won in 1974 and 1975.
- In 1988, Barry Sanders had at least 300 rushing yards in four games. No other college player has matched his record.
- In one amazing 1997 game, Charles Woodson scored on a 78-yard punt return. Then he intercepted a pass in the end zone and caught a 37-yard pass to score a touchdown.
- In 2005, Vince Young became the first college player with more than 3,000 passing yards and 1,000 rushing yards in one season.

In 1906, a college sports committee that later became the NCAA changed the rules. Players were allowed to throw forward passes down the field. To make passing easier, the shape of the ball became oval. Rough play, such as punching and kicking, was not allowed. By 1935, the ball was the size and shape of the modern ball.

Racism affected Black players for decades. From the 1930s until the early 1970s, some teams and schools in the US were segregated. They unfairly kept Black and white students apart and didn't allow Black athletes to play sports. All-white teams such as the University of Alabama refused to play against teams that included Black players.

How national champions are chosen has also changed. Sportswriters used to pick the top teams at the end of the season. In 2015, teams began playing playoff games to crown a champion.

Read on to meet the greatest of all time (G.O.A.T.) college football players. Maybe you think the players should be in a different order. Maybe some of your favorites are missing. Choosing your own favorites is part of the fun!

Early football games, such as this one between Yale and Princeton in 1879, were much rougher than they are today.

NO. 10

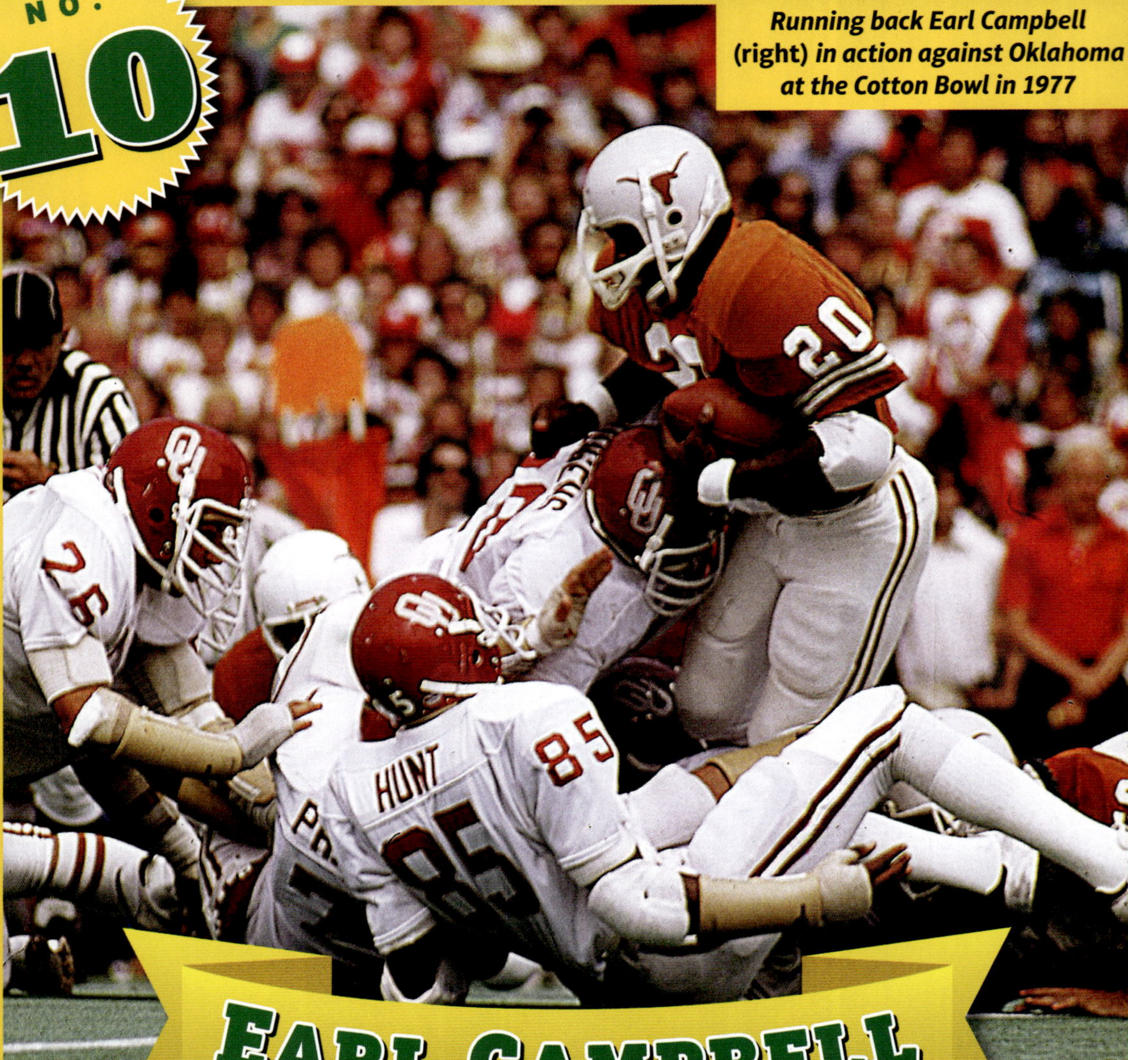

Running back Earl Campbell* (right) *in action against Oklahoma at the Cotton Bowl in 1977

EARL CAMPBELL

UNIVERSITY OF TEXAS (1974–1977)

Running back Earl Campbell started out strong at the University of Texas in 1974. As a freshman, he rushed for 928 yards and six touchdowns. As a sophomore, he ran for 1,118 yards and 13 touchdowns. He helped lead Texas to a 10–2 record that year.

Campbell was big and fast. When he carried the ball, it took several players to tackle him. He used his power to keep moving forward.

In his amazing senior year of 1977, he rushed for 1,744 yards. That set a Southwest Conference record that stood for 16 years. He led the nation in rushing yards and touchdowns with 19. His team had an 11–0 regular-season record.

Earl Campbell set new national records for rushing.

In his four-year college career, Campbell rushed for 4,443 yards. That was the fifth highest total of all time. He also racked up 41 touchdowns.

EARL CAMPBELL FACTS

- Campbell topped 100 rushing yards in a game 21 times and topped 200 yards three times.
- He won the Heisman Trophy in 1977. He was the first player from the University of Texas to win it.
- In his senior year, Campbell was the Southwest Conference Most Valuable Player (MVP).
- As a senior, Campbell averaged 6.5 yards per rushing attempt.

NO. 9

This statue honoring Dick Butkus has stood at the University of Illinois since 2019.

DICK BUTKUS

UNIVERSITY OF ILLINOIS (1962–1964)

Dick Butkus was a big man who played hard for the University of Illinois. At 6 feet 3 (1.9 m) and 237 pounds (107 kg), very few people could remain standing when he tackled or blocked them. He was a two-way player. That means he played both defense and offense. On offense, he played center. On defense, he played linebacker.

Centers snap the ball between their legs to start each play. Then they block opposing players from getting to the quarterback or the running back. Linebackers try to stop opposing players from gaining yards.

Jim Carroll (left) *and Dick Butkus* (right) *warming up before a game in 1964*

In a game against Ohio State in 1963, Butkus set a school record with 23 tackles. That season, Illinois won the Big Ten Conference title. Then, against Washington in the 1964 Rose Bowl, he made an interception late in the game. That sealed the victory for Illinois. Butkus finished his college career with an amazing 374 tackles.

DICK BUTKUS FACTS

- Since 1950, only one linebacker has been voted MVP in the Big Ten. That was Butkus in 1963.
- His 145 tackles in 1963 remained a school record until 1976.
- The American Football Coaches Association named Butkus Player of the Year in 1964.
- A trophy awarded each year to the best college linebacker is called the Butkus Award.

NO. 8

Charles Woodson (center) celebrates a long punt return against Notre Dame in 1997.

Charles Woodson

University of Michigan (1995–1997)

Charles Woodson was a two-way player at the University of Michigan. On offense, he rushed and caught passes. As a cornerback on defense, he stopped passes from getting to wide receivers. He also returned punts. He was the only two-way player to win the Heisman Trophy.

Woodson was named a starter on defense as a freshman. He led the team with five interceptions and was the Big Ten Freshman of the Year. Before the start of his next season, the coach asked Woodson to also play offense. In 1996, Woodson ran about 10 offensive plays each game. He also still played defense.

His best season was 1997. He finished with eight interceptions, the second most in college football that season.

He also scored touchdowns rushing, catching passes, and returning punts. In an amazing game against Ohio State, Woodson scored on a 78-yard punt return and intercepted a pass in the end zone. Then he caught a 37-yard pass for another Michigan touchdown. Michigan was undefeated that season and won the Big Ten Conference title.

Michigan star Charles Woodson was named the Heisman Trophy winner in 1997.

CHARLES WOODSON FACTS

- Woodson ranks second in school history with 18 career interceptions. His eight interceptions in 1997 are also a Michigan record.
- In 1996, Woodson set a school record for breaking up passes with 15. On offense, he caught 13 passes for 164 yards.
- Michigan beat Washington State in the 1998 Rose Bowl. Woodson had one interception and tied a Rose Bowl record by breaking up four passes.
- He finished his college football career with 18 interceptions and 30 passes broken up.

NO. 7

Archie Griffin leaps past defenders in a game against Michigan in 1973.

ARCHIE GRIFFIN

OHIO STATE UNIVERSITY (1972–1975)

Only one player has won the Heisman Trophy twice. Archie Griffin won it in 1974 and 1975. Between 1972 and 1975, the star running back led Ohio State to a record of 40 wins, five losses, and one tie. They won four Big Ten Conference titles. At 5 feet 9 (1.7 m) and 180 pounds (82 kg), Griffin was small for a football player. But he played a very big game.

Griffin had an amazing combination of strength and speed. He could outrun most tacklers. But if they caught up with him, he could push past them.

In only the second game of his freshman year, Griffin rushed for a school record of 239 yards. He topped this the next year with 246 yards in a game against Iowa. As a junior, he rushed for a career-best 1,620 yards and 12 touchdowns. His career rushing total of 5,177 yards set an NCAA record.

Archie Griffin* (center) *had many young fans.

Griffin also has a pair of Silver Footballs. This award is presented every year by the *Chicago Tribune* newspaper to the Big Ten's MVP. Griffin is one of just three players to win it twice.

ARCHIE GRIFFIN FACTS

- Griffin holds the record for most games in a row gaining 100 or more rushing yards. His 31-game streak began in September 1973 and ended in November 1975.
- He was the first player to start in four Rose Bowls in a row.
- Griffin rushed for 1,357 yards and four touchdowns as a senior. He led Ohio State to an 11–0 record.
- When he graduated, he received the NCAA's Top Five Award for excellence in sports, schoolwork, and leadership.

NO. 6

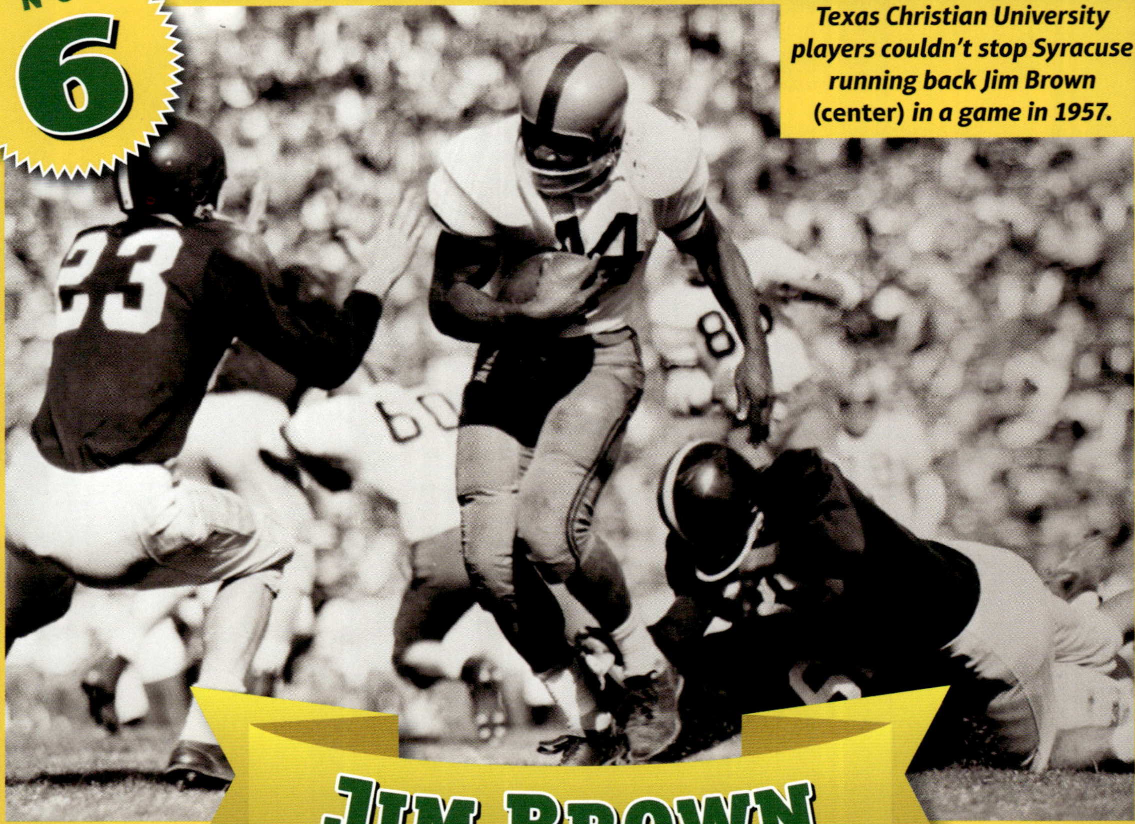

Texas Christian University players couldn't stop Syracuse running back Jim Brown (center) in a game in 1957.

Jim Brown

Syracuse University (1954–1956)

As an athlete, there was nothing Jim Brown could not do. At Syracuse University he was on the football, lacrosse, basketball, and track teams. And he was great at all of them.

The National Lacrosse Hall of Fame considers Brown to be the greatest lacrosse player ever. As a sophomore in 1954, he was the second-leading scorer for the basketball team. That year he also placed fifth in the decathlon at a national college track meet.

On the football field, Brown was an unstoppable running back. In his junior year, his season rushing total was 986 yards.

That was third in the US. He scored 84 points with 13 rushing and one receiving touchdown in eight regular-season games.

Brown also kicked field goals and points after touchdowns for Syracuse. That only added to his scoring. In the 1957 Cotton Bowl against Texas Christian University, Brown scored 21 of Syracuse's 27 points. It was an amazing performance. But Texas Christian held on to win by one point 28–27.

Jim Brown was a top-scoring basketball player at Syracuse in 1954.

JIM BROWN FACTS

- Brown did not play baseball at Syracuse, but he could have. In high school in Manhasset, New York, he was a star pitcher.
- Against Colgate in 1956, he had six touchdowns and made seven extra points. He scored a total of 43 points in Syracuse's 61–7 win.
- Brown is in the College Football Players Hall of Fame, the Pro Football Hall of Fame, and the National Lacrosse Hall of Fame.
- On one great day in May 1957, he won two events at a track meet. Then he changed his uniform and led the lacrosse team to an 8–6 win over Army.

NO. 5

Quarterback Vince Young celebrates a Rose Bowl victory against Michigan in 2005.

VINCE YOUNG

UNIVERSITY OF TEXAS (2003–2005)

Whenever Texas quarterback Vince Young had the ball, there was excitement in the stadium. He was known for making things happen. He could pass and he could run. And that meant he was always a threat to score.

In 2005, Young had his best season. His team had a perfect record of 13–0. He became the first player in NCAA history with more than 3,000 passing and 1,000 rushing yards in the same season.

In the 2006 Rose Bowl, Texas was the underdog against the University of Southern California (USC). The game was one of the greatest in college football. Young completed 30 of 40 passes for 267 passing yards.

Young also rushed for 200 yards against USC. That was a Rose Bowl record for quarterbacks. With 19 seconds left in the game, Young ran eight yards for a touchdown. The score gave Texas the national title and Young was the Rose Bowl MVP.

Texas quarterback Vince Young scores a Rose Bowl touchdown in 2005.

VINCE YOUNG FACTS

- As a sophomore in 2004, Young started every game and led Texas to an 11–1 record.
- Young set a Texas record for a quarterback with 3,127 career rushing yards. He set another record with 37 career rushing touchdowns.
- His overall record as a starting quarterback was 30–2.
- The 2006 Rose Bowl was the most watched college football game in US history. About 35.6 million people tuned in on TV!

NO. 4

Bo Jackson carries the ball against Florida in 1983.

BO JACKSON

AUBURN UNIVERSITY (1982–1985)

Bo Jackson was a great football player, baseball player, and track star. As a running back at Auburn University, he ran for 4,575 total yards and scored 45 touchdowns. He played center field for Auburn's baseball team. His junior year, he had an excellent .401 batting average. On the track team, he ran 100 meters in 10.4 seconds.

In his freshman year, Jackson showed off what a great athlete he was in a famous football game against Alabama. He had been a good high jumper in high school. He convinced his coach to let him leap over the Alabama defensive players to score a touchdown. Jackson completed the play for the win!

Jackson finished his career with an average of 6.8 yards per rush. That set a Southeastern Conference (SEC) record.

Bo Jackson catches a punt in a game against Texas in 1983.

BO JACKSON FACTS

- Jackson missed most of the 1984 season with an injured shoulder. But he came back at the end of the season to be the MVP of the Cotton Bowl that year.
- In 1985, he had four 200-yard rushing games and 1,786 total rushing yards. That was second best in SEC history.
- Jackson won the Heisman Trophy in 1985.
- When Jackson left college, everyone wondered whether he would play pro football or baseball. He played both!

NO. 3

Florida quarterback Tim Tebow runs with the ball against Miami in 2008.

TIM TEBOW

UNIVERSITY OF FLORIDA (2006–2009)

University of Florida quarterback Tim Tebow was a double threat. Like any great quarterback, he could pass. But he could also run the ball like a great running back. In 2007, he became the first NCAA player with at least 20 rushing and 20 passing touchdowns in a season. He was also the first sophomore to win the Heisman Trophy.

In his junior year, Florida lost the fourth game of the season to the University of Mississippi. Tebow promised to help his team do better. They did not lose another game. Tebow led them all the way to the national title.

By the time he graduated in 2009, Tebow had thrown the football for 9,285 yards and 88 touchdowns. He also rushed for 2,947 yards and 57 touchdowns. He held five NCAA records, 14 SEC records, and 28 University of Florida records.

Tim Tebow threw 30 touchdown passes in 2008.

TIM TEBOW FACTS

- Florida went 48–7 with Tebow. In 2008 and 2009, they finished 13–1.
- Tebow is the SEC all-time leader for rushing yards by a quarterback and rushing touchdowns by any player.
- He threw at least one touchdown pass and scored at least one rushing touchdown in 14 games in a row. That was an NCAA record.
- Tebow was more than a great athlete. He also won several college honors for his schoolwork and community service.

NO. 2

Herschel Walker (top) scores his fourth touchdown of the game against Georgia Tech in 1981.

HERSCHEL WALKER

UNIVERSITY OF GEORGIA (1980–1982)

In his freshman year at the University of Georgia, Herschel Walker showed that he was a special player. The running back scored 15 touchdowns and rushed for 1,616 yards. It was an NCAA freshman record at the time. He led Georgia to an undefeated season and the national title. In the Sugar Bowl, he rushed for 150 yards and was named Outstanding Player of the game. Georgia beat the University of Notre Dame 17–10.

Walker was strong and bigger than most running backs. Yet he was incredibly fast for such a big player. His leaping ability was legendary. He could jump over almost any defensive line. And when defenders tried to tackle him, he shook them off like flies.

Herschel Walker carries the ball for Georgia in a 1981 game.

Walker left Georgia to play pro football after his junior year. In his 33 regular-season college games, he scored 52 touchdowns and rushed for 5,259 yards. That's an average of 159 yards per game. It was the highest three-year total ever by a college running back.

HERSCHEL WALKER FACTS

- Walker was a track star in high school. He spent his first spring in college training with the track team. His teammate was future nine-time Olympic gold medalist Carl Lewis.
- Walker placed third in Heisman Trophy voting in 1980 and second in 1981. He won the award in 1982. He is one of only three players with three top-three Heisman finishes.
- He had more than 1,600 yards rushing and 15 or more touchdowns every year he played.

No. 1

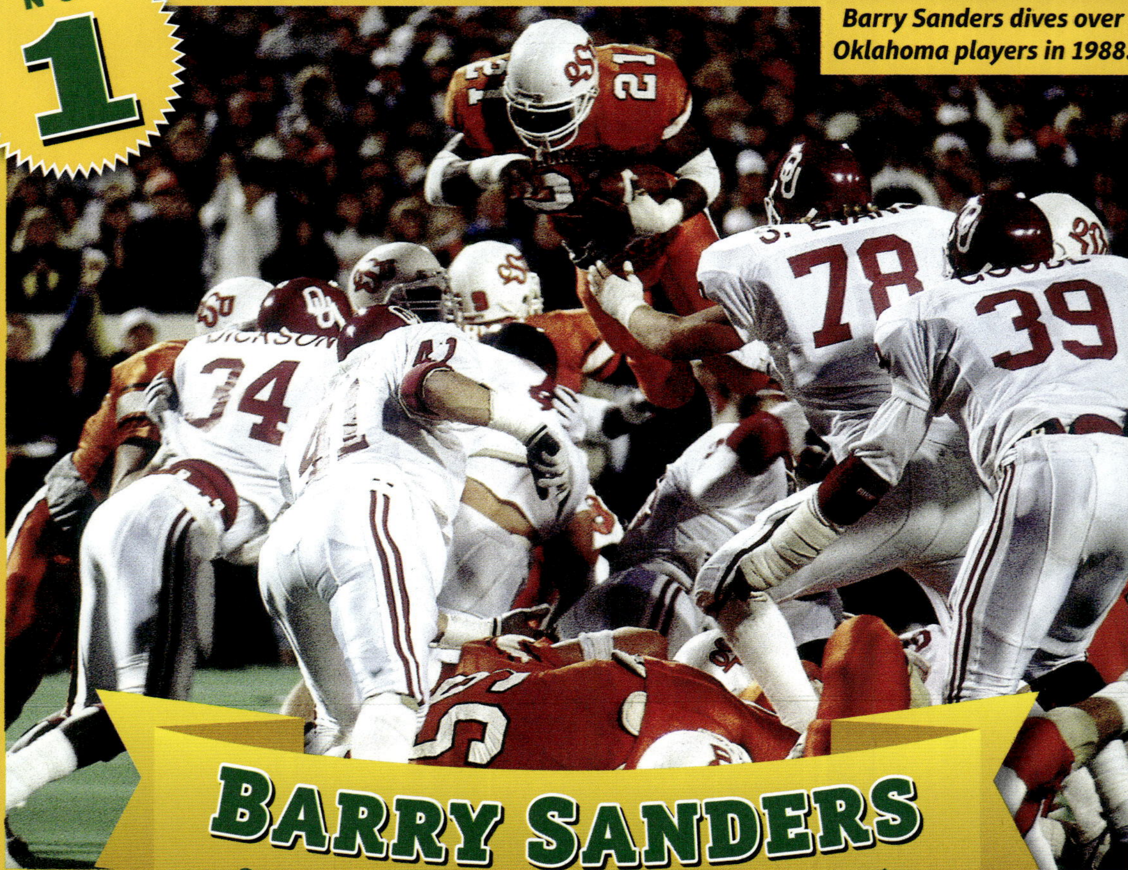

Barry Sanders dives over Oklahoma players in 1988.

Barry Sanders

Oklahoma State University (1986–1988)

In Barry Sanders's first two years at Oklahoma State University (OSU), he was the backup running back to Thurman Thomas. That didn't stop Sanders from showing what a great player he was. In his second year, he dazzled fans on kickoff and punt returns. He led the nation in yards per kickoff return with 31.6.

Sanders was the starter in his junior year. In OSU's first game, Sanders returned the opening kickoff 100 yards for a touchdown. He was just getting started. Sanders's 1988 season was the greatest ever for a college running back.

Sanders set the record for most games in a season with at least 300 rushing yards. He did it four times in 1988. No other running back in NCAA history has had four 300-yard games in their entire career.

Sanders averaged 238.9 rushing yards per game in 1988. He scored 42 touchdowns. He led the nation in rushing yards (2,628), total yards (3,250), and points scored (234). He won the Heisman Trophy and many other awards.

Barry Sanders scores a touchdown against Kansas in 1988.

BARRY SANDERS FACTS

- Sanders set 34 NCAA records. Many have still not been broken.
- His season records of 37 rushing touchdowns and 3.5 touchdowns per game still stand.
- In 1988, Sanders scored three or more touchdowns in five games in a row. That's another record!
- His brother, Byron Sanders, rushed for 1,062 yards for Northwestern University in 1988. Barry and Byron Sanders hold the record for most yards gained by two brothers in a season.

YOUR G.O.A.T.

Football has been played for a long time and has had many great players. Fans don't always agree about who were the greatest players. That's okay! Picking your own amazing players and awesome plays is part of what makes football fun. Your G.O.A.T.s may not be the same as our G.O.A.T.s.

It's your turn to grab a sheet of paper and write down your own list. We ranked these college superstars based on their stats and how they helped their team succeed. Check them out. Then dig deeper. Find out if there are others you think are more G.O.A.T.-worthy.

Is a top 10 list enough? What about a top 15 or top 20? There are no right or wrong answers. It's up to you!

COLLEGE FOOTBALL FACTS

- The longest field goal in college history sailed 69 yards. Ove Johansson of Abilene Christian University kicked it in 1976. Before that, Johansson had only kicked four field goals. He grew up in Sweden and played more soccer than football.
- In 1997, Elizabeth Heaston kicked two points after touchdowns for Willamette University. She was the first woman to score points in a college football game.
- Dominique Davis completed an amazing 36 passes in a row in 2011 for East Carolina University. He set that record over back-to-back games against the University of Memphis and Navy. Nobody else has even come close.
- In a 2016 battle of two super quarterbacks, Baker Mayfield of Texas Tech University faced Patrick Mahomes of the University of Oklahoma.

GLOSSARY

conference: a group of teams that play against one another

decathlon: a contest with 10 athletic events

field goal: a score of three points in football made by kicking the ball over the crossbar

Heisman Trophy: an award given every year to the best college football player

interception: a pass caught by the defending team

linebacker: a defender who usually plays in the middle of the defense

line of scrimmage: an imaginary line that marks the position of the ball at the start of each play

National Collegiate Athletic Association (NCAA): the group that oversees college sports in the United States

punt: when a football player drops the ball and kicks it before it hits the ground

rushing yard: a yard gained on a running play

title: championship

varsity: the top team at a school

LEARN MORE

College Football Hall of Fame
https://www.cfbhall.com

Doeden, Matt. *34 Amazing Facts About Football*. Minneapolis: Lerner Publications, 2024.

Heisman Trophy Winners:
https://www.heisman.com/heisman-winners

Jacobs, Greg. *The Everything Kids' Football Book*, 8th Edition. New York: Simon & Schuster, 2024.

NCAA Football
https://www.ncaa.com/sports/football/fbs

Reeves, Diane Lindsey. *G.O.A.T. College Football Teams*. Minneapolis: Lerner Publications, 2026.

INDEX

PHOTO ACKNOWLEDGMENTS

Photo Credits: Interior; Mtsaride/Shutterstock, interior; robertsrob/ iStockphoto, interior; Yummybuum/Shutterstock, interior; Alex Voylokov/Shutterstock, p. 4; Jamie Schwaberow/Getty, p. 5; Jeff Zelevansky/Getty, p. 7; Stock Montage/Getty, p. 8; Rich Clarkson/Getty, p. 9; Bettman/Getty, p. 10; Michael Reaves/Getty, p. 11; Media News Group/Getty, p. 12; John Biever/Getty, p. 13; Chuck Solomon/Getty, p. 14; Heinz Kluetmeier/Getty; p. 15; Bettman/Getty. p. 16; Rich Clarkson/Getty, p. 17; Bettman/ Getty, p. 18; Rob Gauthier/Getty, p. 19; John Cordes/Getty, p. 20; Tony Tomsic/Getty, p. 21; John Iacono/Getty, p. 22; Bob Rosato/Getty, p. 23; Bob Rosato/Getty, p. 24; Sporting News/Getty, p. 25; Focus on Sport/Getty, p. 26; Richard Clarkson/Getty, p. 27; Doug Hoke/Getty.

Cover: John Raoux/AP